Words Alive!

by DON SMITH and PETER PORGES

SCHOLASTIC BOOK SERVICES

New York Toronto London Auckland Sydney Tokyo

Text copyright © 1979 by Donald Smith. Illustrations copyright © 1979 by Peter Porges. All rights reserved. Published by Scholastic Book Services, a division of Scholastic Magazines, Inc.

12 11 10 9 8 7 6 5 4 3 2 1   1   9/7 0 1 2 3 4/8

Printed in the U. S. A.   01

Words Alive!

PANTS AND GROWLS

Galerius Maximianus, Roman Emperor from A.D. 305 to 311, was not happy when his personal physician converted to Christianity. His co-Emperor, Diocletian, was even less amused, because he was engaged just then in a massive purge of Christians. There was nothing Maximianus could do to prevent the good doctor from being executed. He was condemned to death in A.D. 305.

The doctor's name was Pantaleone, which means "all-lion," and, being lionlike, he was not that easy to kill. The authorities tried drowning him, burning him, throwing him to wild animals, pouring molten lead on him, tieing him to a moving chariot wheel, and putting him to the sword—all to no avail. At last somebody hit on the idea of chopping his head off—and it worked.

Naturally, poor Dr. Pantaleone became a saint and a martyr in the eyes of the persecuted Christians. He was especially revered in Venice, an early stronghold of Christianity. So many boy-children were named after him there that Venetians were eventually nicknamed *pantaleones*.

More than a thousand years after Saint Pantaleone's execution, a kind of comic theater grew up in Italy known as the *commedia dell'arte*. This form of entertainment relied upon a set of stock, clownlike characters. One of these—a Venetian, of course—was called Pantaleone, or Pantalone, or, in English, Pantaloon. Pantalone was a small-time merchant, and invariably an avaricious, suspicious, lascivious old man. His costume was always the same: a tight red vest and tight red breeches. Before long, breeches like these became known as *pantaloons*, in his honor. However ridiculous they might have seemed at first, trousers of this kind were destined to become the almost universal form of male lower-body attire in the Western world.

From pantaloons to pants is but a short step. From "pants" to "panties" is an even shorter one. But we have certainly come a long way from the good Dr. Pantaleone, his Christian convictions, and his conviction as a Christian.

BOYCOTT

The last name of Captain Charles Cunningham Boycott (1832-1897) is a household word today not because he launched a boycott but because he was boycotted himself. As the British manager of the Earl of Erne's estates in County Mayo, Ireland, Boycott's troubles began when he refused to lower the rents of the tenant farmers living on the absentee Earl's property. They were almost starving because of the repeated crop failures of the 1870's. The response of the locals was to ignore Boycott completely. Not only did his tenants refuse to speak to him, but the shopkeepers would not supply his needs. Boycott was so effectively "sent to Coventry," in fact, that he fled home to England in fear of his life. This

first boycott in history was successful, because in 1881 the British Parliament was obliged to pass a land reform bill to settle some of the Irish farmers' grievances. Perhaps we have Irish rebelliousness to thank for the persistence of this tactic of resistance to oppression—and its name—rather than Captain Boycott's obstinacy.

HOBSON'S CHOICE

Hobson's choice is really no choice at all: you must take what is offered or else take nothing. The man who lent his name to this frustrating situation was Thomas Hobson, a seventeenth-century forerunner of Wells Fargo who carried passengers, baggage, and mail from Cambridge to London and back. He also hired out horses to the students of Cambridge University. But since he knew these young men tended to ride his animals too hard, he made it a standing rule that the horses would be hired in strict rotation only, to preserve his best and most popular mounts from exhaustion. In other words, you could not pick the steed you liked best: you took the next in line, noble beast or tattered nag, or you got no horse at all from Hobson. Hertz and Avis, take note.

CURRYING FAVOR

To curry favor is to flatter and fawn on some-one in order to win their friendship or approval. When I was in school it was called playing up to the teacher—and perhaps it still is.

Originally it was not *favor* that people curried, but Favel, who was a horse. To curry a horse, by the way, is very different from currying lamb or beef: it means to comb it and rub it down—to groom it. Anyway, the horse Favel (or Fauvel, as it was sometimes spelled) was the "hero" of a French tale, the *Roman de Fauvel* (1310). Rather like Reynard the Fox, another figure of early French literature, Fauvel was the symbol of cunning and trickery. So grooming or currying Favel came to mean playing an underhanded game, especially by winning favors through flattery and deceit. And over the centuries people forgot all about the story of Favel, and the expression became "currying favor"—which seemed to make more sense.

SILHOUETTE

A silhouette portrait is made by tracing the outline of someone's shadow, then filling in this outline with black. Having a portrait done this way is much cheaper than calling in a painter, and that's why silhouettes used to be very popular. Later, silhouettists were forced out of business by the advent of photography. The man who gave this technique its name was Étienne de Silhouette, an eighteenth-century Frenchman at first identified not so much with cheap portraiture as with *anything* cut-rate—including trousers without pockets!

How did Silhouette thus come to personify cheapness? Well, he was unfortunate enough to be made finance minister in 1759, at a time when France was almost bankrupt because of

the Seven Years' War. Silhouette took his job very seriously, imposing extra taxes on practically everyone, even the nobles. He went so far as to tell King Louis XV to limit *his* spending. His economic measures were so stringent—and hit so many people in the pocketbook—that he was soon dismissed. And so all his plans were reduced to mere *silhouettes*.

GUILLOTINE

The French have their own way of doing most things, and their solution to the problem of executions is typically original. The beheading apparatus known as the guillotine was brought in at the time of the French Revolution of 1789. It was actually introduced as a kinder and more dignified way of sending reprobates into the "next world" than plain old hanging. The man responsible for this humane reform was Doctor Ignace Guillotine of Paris. The inventor of the device itself was another doctor, Antoine Louis, and for a while the thing was called a *louisette* after him. In the end, though, it was Guillotine who gave his name to the sinister contraption. Later, his descendants asked the French government to

change the name, but the authorities refused, telling the family to change *its* name instead. Some people say that Guillotine was guillotined himself, by a sort of poetic justice. Not true: he died in his bed many years later, "executed" by a carbuncle on his shoulder.

"WE CALL IT CHAUVINISM!"

When people talk about chauvinism nowadays, more often than not they mean *male* chauvinism: the belief that men are superior to women, and the behavior resulting from this assumption. Male chauvinists do not want to face the obvious fact that girls can do almost anything boys can do—and quite a few things that they can't. Of course, since most of the power in society has long been held by men, there has been a tendency for this silly and fraudulent theory to become a self-fulfilling prophecy.

"Chauvinism" is the belief that one's own nation, or one's own sex, or one's own anything, is naturally superior to all others, especially when such patriotism is carried to a

17

ridiculous extreme. It was a Frenchman who gave his name to this aberration: one Nicolas Chauvin, a trooper who served in Napoleon's army. Wounded no less than seventeen times, Chauvin was eventually put out to pasture with a miserable two hundred francs a year as veteran's pension and a decorative saber as a souvenir. Another man might have been disillusioned by such high-handed treatment. Not so with Chauvin, who continued to champion Napoleon long after his fall from power and popularity. So high-pitched were his praises for the former emperor that his mad loyalty to this lost cause inspired a whole series of comic plays with Chauvin as the main figure of fun.

Do not jump to the conclusion that because Chauvin was French, the French are any more chauvinistic than anyone else. The British have their own brand of chauvinism, known as "jingoism." The original Jingoists were a minority of English politicians who wanted to fight Russia when she was invading Turkey in 1878. Their marching song was a music-hall ditty of the time which went, "We don't want to fight, yet by jingo! if we do, we've got the ships, we've got the men, and got the money too."

As for home-grown American flag-waving, there is a word for that too: inflated or boastful talk about the United States is known, by reference to the nation's emblem, an eagle, as "spread-eagleism."

PLIMSOLL MARK

Look at any oceangoing ship and you will see a variety of marks on the bow and stern. A set of lines, sometimes with numbers alongside them, serve to measure the ship's draft at any particular time. In other words, they tell us how much of the vessel is under water. These lines are called draft marks. Naturally, the more heavily laden the ship is with cargo, the deeper it sits in the water.

One draft mark is more significant than the others. It is not just a line, but a line with a circle superimposed on it, and it is found not at bow or stern but amidships. This is the Plimsoll line or Plimsoll mark, and it shows the maximum draft permissible for safe loading; if the water level rises above this line in the

dock, it means that the boat is overloaded and will be in danger of being swamped if it runs into heavy seas.

The Plimsoll line must be respected when a ship is being loaded, a rule that has no doubt saved countless sailors' lives. The originator of this safety device was Samuel Plimsoll, member of the British Parliament (1868-1880), a great campaigner for the rights of sailors. In those days unscrupulous shipowners often loaded their cargo boats well beyond safe limits. These men were forerunners of today's criminal landlords who deliberately burn their own property in order to collect the insurance. It was a common practice in the early part of the last century to send heavily insured vessels to sea overloaded. The loss of a ship was often a financial boon to a well-insured owner, while the loss of life involved was a matter of, at most, inconvenience.

It took a long campaign by Samuel Plimsoll, M.P., to finally put a stop to this ruthless racket. The Plimsoll-line rule was made law in Britain by Act of Parliament in 1876, and today nearly all seafaring nations enforce the same convention.

PENNSYLVANIA

The state of Pennsylvania is named not for its founder, the Quaker William Penn, but for that gentleman's father, Admiral Sir William Penn (1621-1670). The elder William Penn was a lifelong supporter of King Charles II of England, and he once loaned the King sixteen thousand pounds. Ten years after his father's death, the younger Penn asked the King to repay this debt to his family in the form of real estate in the New World. William Penn, Jr., was a great believer in religious toleration, and his ambition was to carry out a "holy experiment" by establishing a colony where people could live together in harmony no matter what their religious beliefs.

Charles agreed to the proposal, giving Penn

a charter to "a tract of land in America north of Maryland." Charles further decreed that the future colony should be called Pennsylvania—which means "Penn's woodland"—in honor of the old Admiral.

Penn the younger did not like Charles' name for the place. As a strict Quaker, he felt that such a use of the family name might suggest a most un-Christian pride. He did not hesitate, however, to try and bribe one of the King's under-secretaries into reversing the decision and changing the name to "New Wales."

But the King had spoken, the name stuck, and the state of Pennsylvania, which was to play such an important part in the history of the United States, had come into being. Soon afterward, Penn established Philadelphia as capital of the new state. This time, at least, he had a free hand when it came to naming the place, and "Philadelphia" is derived from the Greek words for "city of brotherly love."

MESMERISM
or "Dr. Mesmer, I...(snore)"

Some birds.of prey immobilize their victims—rabbits or other small animals—by *mesmerizing* them. In other words, they stare at them and hypnotize them into staying perfectly still instead of running away. Then they gobble them up. We also say that a person is mesmerized when he cannot take his eyes off something or someone, just as though he was spellbound—under the spell of some invisible, fascinating force.

The verb mesmerize and the noun mesmerism both come from the name of Franz Anton Mesmer (1734-1815), an Austrian physician who discovered hypnotism without realizing it. Mesmer was also one of the first psychotherapists in history. But posterity has

not done Mesmer justice, because his name has long been synonymous with fraud and quackery.

Mesmer found that he could cure some sick people, whose afflictions ranged from gout to paralysis, by passing magnets over their bodies. He organized group-therapy sessions in which his patients sat around a large tub full of sulphuric acid, clasping magnetized iron bars half immersed in the liquid. Every now and then, one of the participants would go into a sort of hysterical fit and promptly recover from whatever had been ailing him or her.

Mesmer would supervise the proceedings dressed in long, colored robes and brandishing a wand, all of which created a somewhat unscientific atmosphere. After a while, Mesmer came to the conclusion that these arrangements were unnecessary: he only had to touch the sick person, or magnetize a glass of water and have the patient drink it, and they would be cured. One of his students, Chastenet de Paységur, even magnetized trees and encouraged people to come and be healed merely by sitting beneath them.

The sober medical fraternity in Vienna was not impressed by Mesmer's miracle cures, and they denounced him for practicing magic. Undeterred, the doctor moved to Paris, set up a practice, and in no time established a rich and elegant clientele.

At first Mesmer thought that his powers

were astrological in nature—that they were governed by the movements of the stars. Then he decided that some people, like himself, had the capacity to transmit something he called "animal magnetism" to others. This magnetism he looked upon as a "fluid"—a supernatural force that he was somehow able to tap.

Despite his very eminent supporters in Paris, who included Lafayette and Marie Antoinette, Mesmer soon came under attack once again. He was accused of being a charlatan—a con man like those sellers of "snake oil" who used to sell useless remedies to the unsuspecting settlers in the American Wild West. In the end, Louis XVI appointed a team of scientists to look into his seemingly outlandish claims. This committee, which included the American inventor and politician, Benjamin Franklin, and the French chemist, Antoine Lavoisier, dubbed poor Mesmer a phony once again. To make things even worse, the French Revolution of 1789 drove Mesmer into exile in England and Switzerland.

What Mesmer never realized was that his cure was based on hypnotism, much like the cures sometimes performed today by the most respectable of psychiatrists. Even now, scientists cannot agree on the exact nature and causes of hypnosis. All they know for sure is that people *can* be hypnotized. The hypnotized person goes into a kind of trance, rather like Mesmer's patients around the tub of acid; a good hypnotist can get patients into this state very quickly, and once they are in it he suggests to them that they do certain things. Though they will not remember these directions afterward, they will nearly always do what they have been asked. And do you want to know one of the most common suggestions doctors make to hypnotized patients? "Please get better." Believe it or not, they often do just that! Something that old Dr. Mesmer knew well.

MASON-DIXON LINE

The Mason-Dixon line is an imaginary line dividing the North of the United States from the South. When it was first introduced, however, there was nothing imaginary about it. Charles Mason and Jeremiah Dixon were two English surveyors called in to settle a border dispute between the owners of Pennsylvania, the Penns, and the owners of Maryland, the Calverts.

Messrs. Mason and Dixon laid down the exact frontier between the two states in the years 1763-1767, in accordance with the directives of an English court which was supposed to settle the matter. Only later did the Mason-Dixon line come to mean the entire southern perimeter of Pennsylvania—that state's bor-

der with Virginia as well as its border with Maryland. Later still, Mason-Dixon became a convenient way of describing the line of demarcation between the free Northern states and the slave-owning states of the South, the opposing sides in the American Civil War.

SPOONERISMS

Not everyone knows what spoonerisms are, but everyone surely commits them from time to time. Named for the Reverend William Archibald Spooner (1844-1930), onetime Warden of New College, Oxford, a spoonerism is when you get different words or parts of different words in a sentence mixed up. Spooner himself was especially prone to making this kind of mistake. Once, when officiating at the wedding of a young couple, he thought he was helping the groom by telling him, "Son, it is kisstomary to cuss the bride." On another occasion he referred to Queen Victoria as "our queer old dean" instead of "our dear old queen."

Here are a few more samples. See if you can

work out what Dr. Spooner was really trying to say.

"Is the bean dizzy?"

"The cat popped on its drawers."

"The Lord is a shoving leopard."

"I did it in one swell foop."

"I like to ride on a well-boiled icicle."

"The man delivered a blushing crow."

"Young man, you hissed my mystery lecture."

"Mardon me, Padame, this pie is occupied. May I sew you to another sheet?"

During World War I, Spooner is supposed to have announced patriotically, "When our boys come back from France, we'll have the hags flung out."

An interesting fact is some words that everyone uses started out as spoonerisms. There was a time when butterflies were referred to, quite logically, as flutterbies.

SIDEBURNS

Men who let their whiskers grow down the sides of their faces pay unknowing tribute to General Ambrose Everett Burnside. Burnside was not too successful as a military man. As a matter of fact, his career as a soldier was made notable mainly by a series of disasters. During the Civl War, for instance, he decided to dig a tunnel under Confederate lines and blow the enemy up with dynamite. When this harebrained scheme failed he was almost dismissed. But Burnside always enjoyed great popularity, and later he served three terms as Governor of Rhode Island. He was also something of a sharp dresser. The dashing hat he wore into battle became known as a Burnside.

And his sidewhiskers, which he wore in a mutton-chop style all his own, started a craze for "burnsides." The name was soon turned around to "sideburns," because this sounded more like the older names for the same thing, "sidebars" and "sideboards."

AMERIGA, COLUMBIA, ERICKA (or the Good Ole U.S.A.)

The continent of America is named after Amerigo Vespucci (1454-1512), "America" representing a Latinized form of his first name. Vespucci was an explorer in the employ of the famous Italian de Medici family, and historians have long argued over the validity of his claim to fame—and the fame of his name. What is certain is that he did not *discover* America. As everyone knows, Columbus first landed on the island of Hispaniola (now made up of Haiti and the Dominican Republic) in 1492. Vespucci did not reach the New World until 1499. But he was responsible, in the next three years, for exploring about 6,000 miles of the Eastern coastline of South America, especially the mouths of the Amazon and the Rio de la Plata.

The name America was first applied to the continent in Vespucci's honor by the map-maker Martin Waldseemüller, who in 1507 published an atlas called *Introduction to Cosmography*. By this time it was clear that a new continent had been found—and not just another route to the Indies, as Columbus had thought. This added a fourth continent to the three then known: Europe, Asia, and Africa. (Australia was not even sighted by European sailors until about 1600.) As Waldseemüller wrote, since Vespucci had "discovered a fourth part of the world, it should be called, after him, America."

Perhaps this was a little unfair to Columbus. The Spanish, Columbus' original sponsors in his expeditions, kept on using the name "Columbia" right down to the eighteenth century. In the end, Amerigo won out. To quote Victor Hugo, "Columbus could not attach his name to his discovery; guillotine could not detach his name from his invention." As a consolation prize to Columbus though, we do talk about "pre-Columbian America" when we wish to refer to this continent as it was before the Europeans arrived. After all, it would be a bit too confusing to call it "pre-American America."

The claim has been made that even Columbus did not discover America. In fact it is almost certain that Leif Erickson, a Norseman from Iceland, visited North America in the year

1000 or thereabouts, and that the Vikings had landed here even earlier.

In any case, no claim to have discovered America can really compete with that of our native Americans—known as "Indians" only because of Columbus' notion that he had arrived in the Indies by a westerly route. The first "Indians" reached America some time before the year 30,000 B.C., crossing the Bering Strait from Northeast Asia and eventually settling the entire continent, North and South. So the Vikings, Leif Erickson, Columbus, and Amerigo Vespucci were all really nothing but johnnies-come-lately.

PEEPING TOM AND LADY GODIVA

The original Peeping Tom did his peeping in Coventry, England, during Lady Godiva's famous horseback ride through the city's streets in her birthday suit.

Godiva was the wife of Leofric, earl of Murcia, and she lived in the eleventh century. The story goes that Leofric, irritated by his wife's never-ending pleas on behalf of a citizenry overburdened by taxes, sarcastically vowed to give the people some relief if Godiva would ride naked through the streets. He might as easily have said, "I'll do it when the pigs grow wings."

But Lady Godiva took Leofric at his word. Through the crowded marketplace she rode quite naked, though covered by her fabulously long and beautiful hair.

At least, that is the oldest version of the tale. In a later version, dating from the sixteenth century, Lady Godiva orders the townspeople indoors while she goes on her chilly expedition. And it is in this version that Peeping Tom, whose house happens to be strategically placed along Godiva's route, cannot resist un-shuttering his window as she passes by. As punishment, cruel but apt, he is struck blind.

In both versions of the legend, Leofric is honor-bound to remove the heavy taxes from the inhabitants of Coventry. And he does so—except for the tax on horses.

A "Godiva procession" is still held in Coventry every seven or eight years to commemorate the great spirit of sacrifice displayed by Leofric's wife for the sake of the ordinary townsfolk.

PICKLES

There is more to a pickle than the slice of pickled cucumber that goes on your hamburger, although this is what the word means to most Americans. Actually you can pickle almost anything edible simply by preserving it in brine, which is salty water or vinegar. Among the most commonly pickled foods, worldwide, are cabbage, cauliflower, eggs, and fish—especially herring. Great favorites among the British, who are avid pickle-eaters, are pickled walnuts—you eat the shell too, because it gets soft when soaked in vinegar—and a mixed pickle called piccalilli (not to be confused with another British institution, Picadilly).

Probably the first food ever pickled was fish.

The pickling process is supposed to have been invented by a fourteenth-century Dutch fisherman, one Willem Beukelz. "Pickles" is a rather poor attempt by English speakers to pronounce Beukelz's name, which would normally be pronounced approximately "boykells."

Well, that's one theory anyway.

BRITISH BOBBIES

Surprisingly enough, London had very little in the way of policemen until 1829, when Sir Robert Peel passed the Metropolitan Police Act. A conservative politician who later became Prime Minister, Peel already had some experience: in 1814 he had been responsible for introducing a police force in Ireland known as the Royal Irish Constabulary. The main task of this force was to keep the unruly Irish Catholics under the thumb of the Protestant authorities. Peel's men were not too popular among the poorer classes in Ireland, who dubbed them "Peel's Bloody Gang." Peel himself, as defender of Orange (i.e. Protestant) law and order, earned the nickname of Orange Peel.

After Peel returned (with a sigh of relief) to England, and founded London's police force, his men were scarcely more popular among the equally unruly poor of the capital. They were called "Peelers" (as they had been in Ireland), and this label was about as complimentary as other names they were given at the time, such as *crushers* and *raw lobsters*. Why lobsters? Because they were always pinching people. (Policemen are also called coppers because they "cop" people.)

Later on, a little more affectionately perhaps, English policemen were nicknamed bobbies—Bobby being short for Robert (Peel). In recent years the British have grown even more affectionate towards their "law enforcement officers," and they have made a kind of national trademark out of the "friendly bobby." "If you want to know the time," goes a popular song, "ask a policeman." But the British still grumble—as people do all over the world, no matter how honest and fairminded the local cops are—that "When you need them, they're never around. If you don't, they are all over the place."

SANTA CLAUS: THE PEOPLE'S BANKER

Kids used to believe in Santa Claus at least until they were ten or so. Nowadays, three-year-olds will tell you scathingly that "everyone knows Santa Claus is not real—only pretend." Well, I have news for all those diapered doubters: there may not be such a person as Santa *now*, but there was *once!*

The original Santa Claus was Saint Nicholas, a fourth-century bishop of Myra, in what is now Turkey. Nicholas is the patron saint of children—perhaps because he is said to have once brought back to life three little boys who had been killed, salted, and pickled by a butcher who wanted to sell them for bacon. He is also the special saint of many places, including Greece, Sicily, and Russia,

as well as of all sailors, scholars, thieves, and pawnbrokers.

Like all saints in the calendar of the Catholic Church, Nicholas has his own feast day, which is December 6th. It was long the custom in Holland to give children gifts on this day, and New York's Dutch settlers brought this tradition with them to the place they called New Amsterdam. After the British defeated the Dutch and seized New Amsterdam in 1664, they inherited the cult of Saint Nicholas. They rebaptized the city New York and transformed Saint Nicholas' Dutch name *Saint Klaas* into Santa Claus. And they incorporated the benevolent Saint Nicholas into the ceremonies of the English season for giving children presents, which was Christmas.

The real Saint Nicholas was always saving people from misfortune. His best known act of kindness was to give three bags of gold as dowries to the daughters of a poor man, thus making them worth marrying and saving them from the fate of unmarriageable girls—a life of prostitution. These three bags of gold are symbolized by the three gold balls that are seen outside pawnbrokers' shops all over the world. The first pawnbroker to hang out this sign must have flattered himself into thinking he was something of a Saint Nicholas himself for lending money to some poor wretch, too broke to buy food, but with a good coat to hock. (Or perhaps I am forgetting that Nicholas is the patron of thieves—a group that might well be said to include pawnbrokers.)

Santa Claus has all of Saint Nicholas's benevolence. But his long white beard, red coat, pot belly, sleigh, and reindeer were certainly never seen in fourth-century Myra. These embellishments we owe to nineteenth-century New Yorkers, although they have now become a common feature of Christmas lore throughout the English-speaking world, as well as in many other countries.

MAVERICK

A maverick is a loner, an outsider, a non-conformist, a "cat that walks by himself." Why? Well, it's all because Sam Maverick had no taste for cattle ranching.

Samuel Augustus Maverick (1803-1870) was a Texas lawyer who became an owner of livestock quite by chance. A hero of the war for the independence of Texas from Mexico, and a signer of Texas' declaration of independence on March 2, 1836, Maverick was given his herd in payment for a debt in 1845. He hung on to it halfheartedly for ten years, then sold out to one A. Toutant de Beauregard. Maverick's lack of interest in his animals was reflected in the fact that many of his calves had never been branded, and Beauregard's men cheerfully

rounded up *all* unmarked yearlings in the area. Such unbranded stock was already known to all the locals as "Maverick's," and since then, cowboys always refer to unmarked cattle in the same way. By extension, the word *maverick* has come to mean someone who doesn't run with the herd, and who answers to no one.

THE REAL McCOY

So who *was* "the real McCoy"? Answer: Kid McCoy, world welterweight champion from 1890 to 1900. As the song goes, "It was Tiger Wilson versus Kid McCoy..." At that time, prizefighters at the bottom of the ladder of fame would commonly take the name of an earlier champion, much as Houdini took his stage name from a great French magician of the preceding century. Even Jack Dempsey took his professional handle from an earlier namesake, Jack ("The Nonpareil") Dempsey. Anyway, Kid McCoy was top of his profession for so long that a regular horde of emulators were fighting under his name even before he retired, which is why he had to start billing himself as "The *Real* McCoy."

BOWIE KNIFE

Nearly everyone thinks the Bowie knife was invented by Colonel James Bowie (1796-1836), hero and martyr of the Alamo and friend of Davy Crockett. Not so. It was Bowie's elder brother, Regin Pleasant Bowie, who designed the original version of this very popular, two-bladed hunting-knife in Louisiana, in about 1827.

With yet another brother, John, the Bowies had started out in the less than heroic business of slave running. James went on to become a leader of the Texan settlers who eventually drove the Mexicans out of that state and declared it independent. And, even if he did not *invent* the bowie knife, he certainly *used* it

a good deal. One occasion was a duel in Natchez, Mississippi, in which six people were killed and sixteen wounded. Bowie did not die fighting, however. When he was killed at the Alamo he was lying sick in bed.

By the way, another name for a bowie knife is an "Arkansas toothpick."

GALVANI AND HIS FROGS' LEGS

It is amazing how often Batman and Wonder Woman and other superheroes are said to be *galvanized* into action. To galvanize something really means to run an electric current through it, to "electrify" it. It all started with one of the great pioneers in the discovery of electricity, Luigi Galvani, a surgeon and professor of anatomy at the University of Bologna, Italy. Galvani (1737-1798) got quite a shock one day while experimenting with some frogs' legs. Some people say that he wasn't experimenting so much as fixing dinner for his wife—which is quite possible, since Italians love frogs' legs almost as much as Frenchmen and Louisianans do.

Anyway, what surprised Galvani was the

fact that when he touched one of his frogs' legs with a scalpel which he was using to dissect it, it twitched convulsively as though it were alive. This electrical reaction was actually produced by an electric charge passing (via the frog's leg) from the scalpel to another metal object nearby. But Galvani thought the electricity had its source in the leg itself, and he called it "animal electricity." He and his followers continued experimenting for twenty years on this phenomenon, using dead animals of all kinds and even the decapitated corpses of executed criminals.

Galvani's theory was exploded by another electrical pioneer, Alessandro Volta (1745-1827), professor of physics at the University of Pavia, also in Italy. Volta was able to point out the real cause of the jerky behavior of Galvani's bits and pieces of animals. The truth is that contact between two dissimilar metals can generate electricity, a fact that Volta understood much better than Galvani.

Volta's name, by the way, is the source of *volts* as units of electrical measurement. For some reason nearly all the technical terms used in the realm of electricity and its workings derive from the names of the early experimenters in the field. The *coulomb*, a unit of measurement of electric charge, is named for Charles Augustin de Coulomb (1736-1806), once France's superintendent of waters and fountains. One *faraday* equals 96,500

coulombs. The faraday comes from the name of the Englishman, Michael Faraday (1791-1862). Faradays are not to be confused with *farads*, also named for Faraday, which are units of electrical capacity. The *ampere*, a unit of electrical intensity, gets its name from another Frenchman, André Marie Ampère (1775-1836). *Watts*, *kilowatts* and *megawatts* immortalize the memory of the Scottish inventor James Watt (1736-1819). *Ohms*, which measure electrical resistance, are named for the German, George Simon Ohm. And, as though things were not complicated enough, Ohm's name spelled backwards gives us a *mho*, which measures electrical conductance.

No wonder Galvani was a little confused about what was going on when he *faradized* those frogs' legs.

"CUT IT OUT, DR. BOWDLER!"

In 1818, there appeared *The Family Shakespeare*, a ten-volume edition of that immortal Bard's works in which, to quote the editor, "those words and expressions are omitted which cannot with propriety be read aloud in a family." The editor in question was Dr. Thomas Bowdler (1754-1825), a self-appointed guardian of the public morals, a member in good standing of the Society for the Suppression of Vice, and an unflagging opponent of plain language. Shakespeare, Bowdler felt, had been so blinded by the over-tolerant attitudes of the sixteenth century that his plays were peppered with "objectionable" material. Not that he blamed Shakespeare for his indelicacy, exactly; it was just, thanks to the superior wisdom of his own (very Victorian) century, that Bowdler could see where his illustrious predecessor in the world of letters had erred.

Bowdler summed up his philosophy as follows: "Shall I be classed with the assassins of Caesar, because I have rendered these invaluable plays fit for the perusal of our virtuous females? IF ANY WORD OR EXPRESSION IS OF SUCH A NATURE, THAT THE FIRST IMPRESSION IT EXCITES IS AN IMPRESSION OF OBSCENITY, THAT WORD OUGHT NOT TO BE SPOKEN, OR WRITTEN, OR PRINTED, OR, IF PRINTED, OUGHT TO BE ERASED."

Bowdler had started out in life as a doctor, a profession which he entered reluctantly at the bidding of his father. But he had a weak stomach, and the sight of blood made him queasy. Before long he had to give up his medical practice in London. Fortunately for him—and unfortunately for Shakespeare—a good-sized inheritance enabled him to abandon his surgeon's scalpel and begin wielding the censor's scissors instead. By the time he was through with the "foul-mouthed" William Shakespeare, some of the playwright's greatest characters, including Hamlet, Macbeth, and Falstaff, were well-nigh unrecognizable. As for the rollicking Doll Tearsheet, in *Henry IV, Part II*, she was not only laundered, she was totally lost in the wash, never to be seen again.

Bowdler was in tune with the puritanical spirit of his age, however, and his *Family Shakespeare* was a runaway bestseller. Encouraged by this first successful expurgation, he whipped out his trusty eraser again and thoroughly bowdlerized first the Old Testament and then Edward Gibbon's monumental history of the *Decline and Fall of the Roman Empire*. Who knows what other literary masterpieces might have gone the same way if Bowdler had not caught a cold one day, and died of it.

P.S.: A British scholar, Susan Shatto, has recently suggested that the original bowdlerization of Shakespeare was perpetrated not by Thomas Bowdler but by his sister Harriet. If so, why did she not take credit for the job? According to Shatto, the answer is that she was too modest—in both senses of the word. As a genteel middle-aged spinster, Harriet Bowdler was one of those same "virtuous females" who, instead of busily expurgating Shakespeare, should supposedly never have been exposed at all to the Bard's unbowdlerized bawdiness.

LET GEORGE DO IT

When something is particularly hard to do, people often say, "Let George do it!" I doubt many of them know that when they say this, they are quoting Louis XII of France. The George that Louis had in mind was his lifelong supporter and right-hand man, Georges d'Amboise (1460-1510), cardinal and chief minister of the French state. "He can do it," Louis used to say. "He's the man of the age." And he was probably right, because d'Amboise, a man of many talents and a true "Renaissance man," managed to combine the functions of military strategist, economist, jurist, diplomat, and priest, apparently with-

out effort. So next time you have to take the garbage out, and the task seems overwhelmingly difficult, don't forget to say, "Let George do it." Maybe, if a George happens to be nearby, you'll be spared.

DERRICK
or "Hang It All, Sir!"

"A contrivance or machine for hoisting heavy weights"—that is the dictionary definition of a derrick. Usually we associate the word with oil rigs. Originally, however, the contrivance so named was a more sinister one: the gallows invented in the seventeenth century by Godfrey Derick, a famous (or infamous?) hangman at Tyburn prison near London. And thereby (no pun intended) hangs a tale.

Convicted of rape, a capital offense, Derick was pardoned by Robert, Earl of Essex, on condition that he take the unpopular job of executioner. Essex was then the favorite of Queen Elizabeth I, but he later fell from grace. He plotted a comeback to court and to the

Queen's good graces, but his plot backfired and he was condemned to death for treason.

By an irony of fate, it fell to Derick to dispatch his former protector into the next world—though by beheading, not hanging, because hanging was considered beneath the dignity of noblemen. According to an old English ballad, Essex then addressed Derick thus:

"Derick, thou knowest at Calais I saved
Thy life lost for a rape there done.
But now thou seest myself is come.
By chance into thy hands I light.
Strike out thy blow [i.e. make it quick] that I
    may know
Thou Essex loved at his goodnight."

Far from "striking out," Derick, who was a better hangman than a headsman, made a bad mess of the job, and it took him three blows of the axe to separate Essex's head from his body.

Maybe it is nobler to be beheaded, but I think I would rather have been one of the three thousand unfortunate souls hanged by Derick in his long career in the "detestable office of executioner."

MALAPROPISMS

Being something of a snob, Mrs. Malaprop liked impressing her friends. She hated to use a short word if she could use a long one instead. Unfortunately for her, she always got her long words hopelessly mixed up. No doubt it was an *alligator* she had in mind when she called someone as "headstrong as an allegory on the banks of the Nile." And what do you think she meant by complimenting someone else for being "the very pineapple of politeness"? The very *pinnacle* of politeness, perhaps.

Sometimes, though, things were still not very clear even when you had worked out what Mrs. Malaprop was *trying* to say. Once she announced: "If I apprehend anything in the

world, it is the use of my oracular tongue, and a nice derangement of epitaphs." What she meant was: "If I comprehend anything in the world, it is the use of my vernacular tongue, and a nice arrangement of epithets." Any the wiser? No, because the thing would still have to be put into plain English, thus: "If I understand anything in the world, it is the proper use of the common language, and adjectives put in their proper place."

Mrs. Malaprop was certainly no pineapple of plain speaking. And her name has become synonymous with "pomposity coupled with an inexact choice of words." Mrs. Malaprop is a character in *The Rivals*, a play by Richard Brinsley Sheridan (1751-1816). But Sheridan was not the first to get a laugh from this kind of gag. Shakespeare, who wrote most of his plays in the sixteenth century, has a character named Constable Dogberry, in *Much Ado About Nothing*, who was forever committing malapropisms, as when he said, "All comparisons are odorous." What did he mean to say?

Here are a few more malapropisms. See if you can correct them.

—"His conjuring tricks are incredulous."

—"It was a great humility to be fired the first day on the job."

—"Theseus got lost in a labrador and could not find his way out."

—"Chicken pox is an infantry disease."

BLOOMERS

Everybody has heard of bloomers, and the word still has a vague aura of sinfulness about it. But very few people, except those old enough to remember the time when they were last in fashion, can say exactly what they look like.

In the last century, when bloomers were first worn by women, they were denounced as an affront to decency in countless Sunday sermons. Wearing them became the badge of the liberated women of that time—a challenge to the manmade rule that females could not wear pants of any kind. For bloomers were billowing, Turkish-style trousers drawn tight at the ankle. They were worn beneath a short skirt and accompanied by a loosely fitting blouse.

It was the militant feminist, Amelia Jenks Bloomer (1818-1894), who gave her name to this shocking outfit, although she was not the first person to sport such attire. Credit for that must go to Mrs. Elizabeth Smith Miller. It was Mrs. Miller's cousin, another feminist and suffragette (that is, a campaigner for women's right to vote—a right not won until 1928) who told Amelia Bloomer about bloomers. Amelia proceeded to stomp from coast to coast, publicizing the new costume, writing articles about it, and championing women's right to wear them.

By the turn of the century, women were not only wearing bloomers, they were wearing bloomers and—horror of horrors!—riding bicycles at the same time. Later still, a version of bloomers came in for schoolgirls to wear during phys ed classes. The truth is, despite the outcry against them, bloomers were always a very modest form of attire, and far more practical than ornamental. Because of their fundamental unattractiveness, they never lasted as a fashion. Even Mrs. Bloomer lost interest in the question eventually. As for those who had been shocked by bloomers, they went off in search of something else to be shocked about. And you can be sure they eventually found it.

TEDDY'S TEDDY

Teddy is short for Theodore, and teddy bears are so named for President Theodore Roosevelt. Roosevelt was a passionate big-game hunter, but when it came to shooting a small brown bear that had been knocked on the head and tied to a tree, he had no stomach for the job.

Roosevelt had been invited to Mississippi to hunt bears along the Little Sunflower River, but there were few bears around, and the locals felt that he would be unhappy if he did not bring back some kind of trophy. So, the one bear that could be found was captured and set up for him as a sitting target. But Teddy Roosevelt was not a man to indulge in such

unsportsmanlike behavior, and he told his hosts to set the animal free.

What happened next was that *Washington Post* artist Clifford K. Berryman made this incident the subject of a famous cartoon. Then, in 1902, a Brooklyn toy manufacturer named Morris Michtom made the very first "teddy" bear out of brown plush. That original may be seen today in the Smithsonian Institution, in Washington, D.C. The millions upon millions of cuddly bears sold since have made the teddy into the most popular toy of the twentieth century. Every kid loves his teddy, and some people, especially female film stars, keep their teddies as sleeping companions until they (the film stars, that is, not the teddies) are old and gray. Don't ask me why, because I don't know.

THE HERO OF SANDWICH

One day in 1762, in the wee hours of the morning, John Montagu, Fourth Earl of Sandwich, was overcome by hunger pangs. So engrossed was he in his game, however, that he had no wish to leave the card table. "I say, my man," said the Earl to his valet, "be a good chap and fetch me a bite to eat. I haven't the room for a plate what with all these chips, so just bring me some slices of cold roast beef—thick ones, mind you—and wrap them up in bread for me, eh what! Ah simply can't bear gettin' the old fingers greasy, if you follow my meaning."

And that was the first time in history anyone ever ordered a sandwich. Not the last, though. The sporting Earl had started a fad which soon took fashionable London by storm, and the "quick lunch" (or "quick breakfast"?) had come into being. A contemporary of Sandwich's, Gibbon, describes the sight of "twenty or thirty of the first men in the kingdom supping at little tables upon a bit of cold meat or a Sandwich" as "truly English." I wonder how many sandwiches have been eaten since? Quite a few—especially when you include all those heros, submarines, hoagies, and of course the n billion hamburgers McDonald's has sold since their fast-food chain started in 1947.

Yes, the old Earl definitely started something. Incidentally, the Sandwich Islands (Hawaii) were also named after him, because Captain James Cook, the first European to get there, happened to be working for the Earl at the time. As head of the British Admiralty during the American Revolution, Sandwich was responsible for outfitting Cook's historic expedition to the Pacific.

Aside from these two claims to fame—the roast beef sandwich and the Sandwich Islands—John Montagu was not so much famous as *infamous*. A near-parody of the decadent aristocrat, Sandwich had few virtues and many vices, gambling being the least of these. As head of the British Navy he was accused of taking graft. He was a notorious womanizer and, in the view of most of his countrymen, an absolute cad. To cap it all, he

used to worship not God, but the Devil, in company with his fellow Satanists in the "Hellfire Club," a group of jaded lords whose unsavory pastimes were "quite shocking" to the majority of Englishmen.

Of course, people are sometimes shocked only because they want to be, and when we read today of the weird doings of the Hellfire Club, we are reminded of nothing so much as the silly secret ceremonies of college fraternity houses. I can't help feeling the Earl of Sandwich was a bit of a sheep in wolf's clothing. Perhaps it is no coincidence that his only legacy to us was that mundane and most respectable affair,—"... slices of roast beef wrapped in bread, eh what!"